Origins

The Balloon Team

Chris Powling ■ Jonatronix

OXFORD
UNIVERSITY PRESS

In this story ...

Max

Cat

Ant

Tiger

Flying a hot air balloon ...

A hot air balloon is a balloon filled with hot air!

Air and wind push the balloon along.

Hot air makes the balloon rise.

Gas burners keep the air hot.

Bags of sand stop the balloon from floating too high.

The pilot steers the balloon.

Chapter 1 – The big idea

The children were lying on the grass in Cat's back garden. They were staring up at the sky, trying to pick shapes out of the clouds.

Max thought he saw a car. Tiger saw a bike. Cat saw a face and Ant saw a dog.

Just then, something passed over them, blocking their view of the clouds.

"Wow!" said Tiger. "A hot air balloon."

"Cool!" said Max.

They watched the balloon drift slowly across the sky. It was a splendid sight.

"I wish we had a hot air balloon," sighed Cat. "Then we could see the clouds up close."

"Why don't we make one?" suggested Tiger.

"Don't be silly, Tiger," said Cat. "How can we make something that size?"

"We don't have to," said Tiger. "Let's make a micro-balloon!"

Now that was an idea.

"What do you think, Ant?" said Max. "Can it be done?"

"Well," said Ant. "The technology is fairly basic ..."

"Great," said Tiger, jumping to his feet. "Let's get started."

Chapter 2 – Do-it-yourself

The plan was simple enough. Ant drew a picture of their balloon to scale.

Max, Cat and Tiger went into the house to collect all the things they thought they would need.

Max found a paper cup that could be used as a basket.

Cat found a balloon left over from her birthday. She blew it up and tied it with a peg.

Tiger found a dish cloth that could be used to hold the balloon in place.

Then the real work began. They turned the dials on their watches and ...

It took all morning, but finally their balloon
was finished. It looked amazing. It looked
splendid. It looked *real*.

Chapter 3 – Up, up and away!

"Everyone in," said Max.

"Are you serious?" Ant asked.

"Of course he's serious!" said Tiger. "It's a balloon, isn't it? And balloons are built to *fly*!"

"I thought we were only making a model!"

"It's better than a model," said Cat.

"Yes, but ..."

"Don't worry, Ant," said Max. "We've built it well. It will be OK."

"Yes, but ..."

"And there's plenty of room for all of us," Cat assured him.

"But ..."

"Come on," Tiger said. "Let's go!"

Ant did not want to let the others down. So, with a big sigh, he climbed in.

Tiger untied the string that was holding them to the ground. As soon as they were free, a gust of wind picked them up and lifted them into the air.

"Yippee!" Max, Cat and Tiger all cheered.

"Yeah," said Ant, in a much smaller voice.

The balloon went
higher and higher.
They sailed over
Cat's back garden, then
out towards the park.

"See?" hooted Tiger.
"Is this cool or what?"

Ant just gulped.

Chapter 4 – Kite fright

They flew up and out across the park.

"Right, Ant," said Cat. "How do we steer this thing?"

"Steer?" said Ant. "You can't steer."

"*What?*" cried the others together.

"A real hot air balloon has gas and fire and a proper pilot to make it go the right way. This is just a model." The others looked horrified. "That's what I was trying to tell you before we took off ..."

At that moment, something darted across the sky in front of them. *Whoosh!*

"What was that?" said Tiger, looking over the side.

A big, colourful object shot past them making the balloon wobble.

"It's a kite!" Max exclaimed. "Watch out, everybody. If we get tangled up in its tail, it could drag us down!"

The kite dipped and swirled towards them. It whizzed dangerously close.

"Look," said Tiger. "Someone's steering it from the ground."

Tiger leaned over the side for a closer look. This made the cup tilt and Tiger nearly fell out.

"Aaggghh!" screamed Tiger.

"Tiger!" screamed Cat.

Tiger managed to grab one of the ropes dangling from the side of the balloon. It stopped him falling. Max and Ant grabbed Tiger's leg.

"Quick," cried Max. "Pull him up!"

Tiger looked very pale when he was dragged back in. "Thanks," he said, in a whisper.

"Well done, crew!" said Max, wiping his brow.

But they didn't have any time to relax. Another gust of wind lifted the balloon higher in the sky. It pushed them out of the way of the kite, out of the park and out towards the city ...

As they sailed across the sky, Cat thought she heard something.

She cupped her hand to her ear. "Can you hear that?" she asked.

The others strained to listen. Along with the whooshing of the wind they could make out a soft beating noise. This was followed by a loud squawking.

"Oh, no," yelled Max. "Birds!"

"Crows!" Ant corrected.

The sky darkened as they were suddenly surrounded by wings, beaks and claws all swooping out of the sky.

"Don't let them peck the balloon!" cried Ant. "It will burst!"

"Everyone shout as loudly as you can!" ordered Max.

The micro-friends screamed and shouted. Tiger flashed the torch from his watch at the birds. Finally the crows flew off, scattering feathers behind them.

Chapter 5 –
The NICE skyscraper

The balloon sailed higher, straight into a thick cloud.

"Well, you wanted to get a closer look at the clouds, Cat," said Max.

"Not this close," moaned Cat.

Just then they heard a rumble.

"Uh, oh," said Ant.

"What do you mean, *uh, oh*?" wailed Tiger. "What now?"

"That sounds like thunder," said Ant. "This is a rain cloud."

"We have to get this balloon down," cried Max. "Ant, think!"

"OK," said Ant. "We'll have to let some air out."

"Impossible," said Cat. "We'll spin out of control and crash."

"Maybe not," explained Ant. "Not if we let the air out slowly."

"Can you do it, Ant?"

"I can try, Max. But we'll have to work as a team."

Ant pushed the ends of the peg together and the air hissed slowly out.

Max and Tiger tried to keep the balloon steady. They threw their weight from one side of the cup to the other and tugged down on the strings that tied the balloon in place.

Cat used the compass on her watch to navigate and tell them which direction to go in.

Max and Tiger shifted their weight and the balloon tilted to the right. Ant let some more air out and, bit by bit, they began to sink.

Down they went until, at last, they were beneath the cloud.

Then, looming in front of them, was a wall of glittering glass windows. It was a skyscraper – the NICE building – the tallest building in town.

"We'll never clear that," wailed Tiger. "We'll be splattered!"

Ant concentrated hard. He let some more air out, quickly this time. The balloon sank fast.

Cat grabbed hold of a rope and helped to guide the balloon. They skimmed past the NICE building missing it by millimetres!

Just then, *WHOOSH!* They hit an air current. "This is it!" cried Ant. "Hold on!"

The air current carried them up again. The balloon rocked and swayed then the air current pushed them back in the direction of the park.

"We're safe!" said Cat.

As they came towards Cat's garden, Ant let out more of the air. They drifted gently down. The balloon bumped across the ground and finally came to a stop. The cup tipped up and the children tumbled out, safe at last.

"What a team!" Max whooped.

For other great team adventures read

Divided We Fall

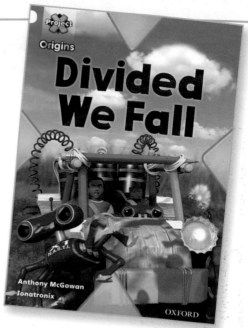

and

Fee Fi Fo...Mum!

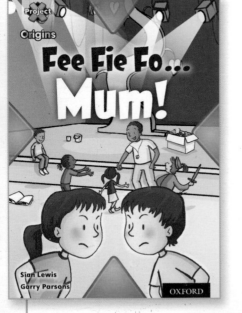